A Guidebook

I do not recall any book being p̶... ̶c̶lassified as a guidebook for reading and studying the Bible though su̶... ̶o̶ok has been needed for years. John Eddins has given us some excellent guidance in the study of the Bible. It is a book that will be of tremendous help to Sunday School teachers, the ordinary reader, and ministers as well.

Dr. T.C. Smith, Professor of New Testament and Greek,
Author of *The Broadman Bible Commentary:* Acts, *How We Got Our Bible,
Jesus and the Gospel of John* and *Reading the Signs*

Dr. John Eddins, a student of the Bible more than a half a century and a Professor of Theology for forty-four years, in this little book identifies what may be the number one barrier blocking the spiritual growth and development of Christian churches and disciples for two millennia. He writes, "Jesus, the Teacher, gave first place to the education of his Apostles and disciples. We have passively accepted what trickles down from others as all we need and as genuine Christian education."

He not only identifies the problem but offers this guidebook for reading and studying the Bible as the solution. Heed what he writes and begin the adventure in Bible Study that will make your life as a Christian disciple richer and fuller.

Dr. Denton Coker, Professor of Christian Education

With scholarly background in the teaching of theology and Biblical languages, the author packages his academic experience in a very understandable and practical manner. This text is both a guidebook for Biblical study and a primer for Christian theological reflection. In a readable, sensible and useful fashion John Eddins provides a Biblical road map that is of value to lay persons and Christian educators as well.

Dr. Thomas H. Graves, Professor of Philosophy of Religion
and President of Baptist Theological Seminary at Richmond, Virginia

Few persons are as qualified to write such a volume as Dr. John Eddins. During six decades he has taught the Bible in his seminary courses and, concurrently, served as interim pastor of churches in which he taught biblical studies to groups of various sizes. This volume has been presented, refined, and revised in light of those discussions with various audiences. Any serious student of the Bible will find this volume immensely helpful.

Dr. Morris Ashcraft, Professor of Theology,
Author of *The Broadman Bible Commentary:* Revelation,
The Will of God and Christian Faith and Beliefs

A GUIDEBOOK FOR
READING AND STUDYING THE BIBLE

JOHN WILLIAM EDDINS, JR.

*A Gift to Stan Hastey
Thanks for keeping the Baptist
vision alive and well and for
your friendship!*

*Always love,
John*

April 30, 2005

Published by John William Eddins, Jr.
DBA Frisco Enterprises

ISBN: 0-9760993-0-6 (pbk.)

Library of Congress Control Number: 2004115948

Subjects: Bible, Religion, Revelation, Christianity, Theology, Systematic Theology,
Dogmatics, Philosophy, Science, History, Literature, Exegesis, Hermeneutics, Methods

Unless noted, Scripture quotations are from the Revised Standard Version of the Bible,
copyrighted 1946, 1952, © 1971, 1973.

Eddins, Jr., John William   1926–
A Guidebook for Reading and Studying the Bible

Published by John William Eddins, Jr.
DBA Frisco Enterprises
9984 Fairway Villas Lane
Pensacola, FL 32514-2603
2005

Printed in the United States of America
by Printing Services, Inc.
4109 Jacque Street, Richmond, VA 23230
2005

DEDICATION

A Guidebook for Reading and Studying the Bible

is dedicated to everyone who seeks

to know, to worship and to serve God

privately and publically

and, in particular, the God who is love

revealed in Jesus of Nazareth.

CONTENTS

Contents

PREFACE

An encouraging challenge from a good friend is not easy to dismiss. An unforgettable request came to me from Dr. Denton R. Coker, a former seminary colleague, following a Sunday School class meeting in January 2003. While discussing and lamenting the scarcity of effective guides to constructive study of the Bible, Denton said, "John, you are the person to write such a guide, will you write one?" Almost in a state of shock, I replied that I would write one if he would make suggestions, no holds barred, and help me with proofreading and other matters. Professor Coker and I have often taught the Friendship Sunday School Class of senior adults at the First Baptist Church of Pensacola, Florida. He suggested that I teach the text of the proposed guidebook to the Friendship Class and discover its merits and demerits. Approximately one hundred members read the manuscript, attended eight classes and responded to an evaluation form. *A Guidebook for Reading and Studying the Bible* is a direct result of Dr. Coker's challenge and our shared desire to encourage and to assist others in helpful ways to read and to study the Bible.

This guidebook is addressed to all who read the Bible casually, devotionally or in an intensive study. The goal is to provide a short constructive guide rather than a polemical or apologetic book about the Bible. This is a "how to go about it" project rather than a formal theological treatise. However, my theological foundations and views are often expressed. *Specifically, my goal is to make available a cluster of useful tools including a helpful plan for ways to read and to study the Bible.* Everyone views life from a different perspective and with different goals. No one, except God, knows reality exactly as it is since all humans are both finite and flawed.

The biblical perspective is that of a comprehensive narrative over a period of approximately two thousand years. The Bible is a collection of "faith-witness narratives." These are narratives written by people who believe in God. When the Bible was canonized, the churches accepted the Bible as their primal document for faith and practice. These faith-witness narratives became the context and norm for Christians in their interpretations of other faith-witness narratives. The Epistle to the Hebrews describes in chronological sequence some outstanding men and women of faith in God (Heb. 11:1-40). These spiritual giants are a part of the biblical narrative which is the context for the normative (L. *norma*, rule or standard) narrative of the revelation of God in Jesus Christ. Their lives are witnesses to faith in God through their words, deeds and deaths. Some of their writings, e.g., the Psalms of David, are a part of the Bible.

This project is challenging and adventurous to me in the context of fifty-five years as a Christian minister and forty-four years as a teacher of Christian theology in seminaries, divinity schools, colleges, universities and churches. The education of Christian leaders and other Christians in the biblical texts, their doctrinal and ethical meanings and their relevance to the Christian Faith (religion) is fundamentally flawed in many programs, old and new. To address this sixteen hundred year tragedy in Christian education, we must reaffirm the old programs which are sound and constructive. Then, we need to read and to study the Bible with new approaches, new information, new ideas and new guidebooks. My hope is that the readers of this book will be enabled and encouraged to have a more adequate understanding of and appreciation for the Bible.

The Bible, as a book and in its own words, is not addressed specifically to Christians, Jews or any particular religion, race or nation. However, many books in the Bible are addressed specifically to individuals, Israel, other nations, Christians and churches. The Bible begins with God, creation and humankind and it continues with its primary concern for the welfare and redemption of all people and all creation. The Bible is a unique gift to all people. It is your book and you are free to read and to study the Bible, without fear, on any topic or subject of interest to you.

Personal pronouns are used throughout the book since this guide is a "person to persons" presentation. Plural personal pronouns (we, you, your, they, them, their, our) are used to avoid unnecessary and inaccurate distinctions of gender in the third person singular (he, she, it) in English. He, she or it is used when the singular pronoun in the third person is important for clarity, accuracy and meaning. The current use of the word "Bible" as an adjective is avoided since it is grammatically incorrect and it may diminish the singular concept of the Bible.

In studying the Bible, I often use the present tense when describing past events such as the life and teachings of Jesus. There is a profound difference between Jesus said "follow me" and Jesus says "follow me." Sometimes the use of the present tense is more relevant than the past tense.

The contents of this book are my sole responsibility. I am profoundly indebted to Professor Coker, members of the Friendship Sunday School Class and the Chapel Sunday School Class, Laurie E. and Norman Thrash, Professor Thomas H. Graves, President of the Baptist Theological Seminary at Richmond, Toni Clevenger, Martha Dickson and Jill Findley for extensive assistance. Other beloved colleagues and cherished friends who proofread the manuscript and offered helpful suggestions and encouragement are Dr. Morris Ashcraft, Dr. T.C. Smith, Dr. T. Furman Hewitt and Donna W. Hewitt, Dr. Roger Mott, Dr. Betty Pugh, Dr. David A. Eddins, John Divers, Kristi D. Tillett, Debra E. McGuire, CDR, CHC, USN, Alton and Willowdean Strickland, Bernie and Marie Henderson and especially Nita Doolin, Sales/Production Liaison, Printing Services, Inc., Richmond, Virginia. The superb cover was designed by Katherine Lawton, Printing Services, Inc.

More than fifty years ago a sermon entitled "Your Bible" was preached in the Chapel at The Southern Baptist Theological Seminary in Louisville, Kentucky by Dr. William O. Carver, Professor of Missions. Dr. Carver said, "Your Bible is that portion of the Scriptures which has penetrated your mind and heart and by which you live daily." Then, I heard him ask a question which challenges and troubles me frequently. "How large is your Bible?"

The focus of this book is on reading and studying the Bible. Jesus teaches, "Ask, and it will be given you; seek, and you will find; knock, and it will be opened to you" (Mt. 7:7). Open your Bible, select your tools, make your plan and ask God to help you read, study and pray until you can say, "This is my Bible!"

John William Eddins, Jr.
Pensacola, Florida
January 2, 2005

I
INTRODUCTORY REMARKS

Reading the Bible is something many of us do for a variety of reasons. However, reading the Bible and understanding what we read is not as simple as it may seem. In fact, the Bible is an exceedingly complex book. It is a diverse collection (Gk. *ta biblica*, the books) of many writings. It is easier to read the Bible and understand it if we give attention first to our perspectives; second, to our assumptions about the Bible; and third, to the tools we bring to the Bible.

One helpful way to read and to study this guidebook is to use a suitable notebook as a workbook and diary in response to the table of contents, preface, introductory remarks and other parts of this book. You may be surprised as you rediscover and reaffirm what you already know and you may become interested in new information and ideas. Keep this record of your journey in your study of the Bible. Serious study of the Bible is sometimes an arduous and mind-stretching endeavor. As in all serious quests for truth and knowledge, focused mental effort and persistent determination are essential in reading and studying the Bible. Fortunately, you may be surprised often by a sense of joy and satisfaction in your earnest quest for information, truth and meaning.

The Bible is often read with a random approach in which one goes from one verse, one passage and one book to another looking for something. This approach may be interesting but it is inadequate for serious study. A random approach is frequently used to search for proof-texts to prove a belief or theory to which the reader is already committed and is seeking biblical support and authority. The proof-text method may prevent a reader from learning what the text actually means by imposing on the text different ideas and meanings. With a proof-text method a reader can use the Bible to prove, to his or her satisfaction, almost any opinion or point of view. Proof-texts alone actually reveal or prove little beyond what a reader already believes and knows. There is a profound difference between finding a proof-text and seeking the meaning of a text.

A comprehensive approach to the study of the Bible includes studying each verse, passage and book of the Bible in its own context and in the context of other relevant passages and groups of books in the Bible (Law, Prophets, Writings, Gospels, Epistles, etc.). In this approach readers have a high regard for the integrity of the overall historical and chronological structure of the Bible as far as it can be known. In this manner, we go to the Bible to discover what the text says and means, as far as this is possible, rather than what we want it to say, mean and prove.

One's personal approach to reading and to studying the Bible determines in large measure the quality of the results and benefits. What is your attitude toward the Bible? Non-Christians often ignore and avoid the Bible as being irrelevant. Many Christians also avoid the Bible, that is, some of us often create barriers in our minds which hinder us from reading and studying the Bible. The disposition which leads to truth, knowledge, wisdom and understanding is one of passion and openness without fear as our "faith seeks understanding" (Augustine of Hippo, 354-430) of God and ourselves. The Bible does not yield its messages and its blessings easily to negative attitudes shaped by ignorance, dogmatism, subversion, manipulation or unbelief. Describe in your notebook your attitude toward the Bible and seek out the sources of any negative attitudes toward reading and studying the Bible and deal with these negative attitudes now and in the future.

This self-examination may enable you to cleanse your mind and heart of obstacles and it may encourage you to permit the Bible to teach you the meaning of its texts rather than for you simply to find what you seek. An open and humble attitude is one the Holy Spirit respects and works with in enabling you to interpret the Bible adequately. No one interprets the Bible perfectly. The meaning of a biblical text is not completely self-evident to any person. Each interpreter is exceedingly subjective and needs the guidance of the Holy Spirit for adequate knowledge and understanding. When you open the Bible, examine your attitude as you read and study, then open your mind and heart to the mind of Jesus Christ and the wisdom of the Holy Spirit.

The "circle of faith" in which each person lives is a helpful analogy used by Paul Tillich (1886–1965). Awareness of one's circle of faith is crucial for studying the Bible. The circle of faith is distinctively different for Jews, Christians, Muslims, secularists, atheists, agnostics and every other perspective. For Christians, the Lord Jesus Christ is the center of the circle of faith. Each Christian stands with Jesus Christ in a unique circle of faith. Perhaps, "arcs of faith" may be a helpful and supplementary analogy since circles include and exclude, whereas arcs encourage inclusiveness and relationships. Some weaknesses of the "arcs of faith" analogy are that it may be somewhat awkward and it may be more difficult to visualize and to apply. However, the "circle of faith" analogy is widely accepted as a good place to begin. Therefore, I use it throughout the book. The biblical perspective is clearly relational and inclusive.

Many Jews, for example, take the Promise to Abraham or the Covenant of the Law given to Moses as the center of their circle of faith. Notice that each person's circle of faith becomes a different formative and shaping factor in reading, studying and interpreting the Bible. This is not surprising and we should not be too alarmed when other Christians and non-Christians have widely different interpretations of the same biblical passage. We cherish the freedom to have our own interpretations and graciously grant that same freedom to all others. Make certain that you are clearly and explicitly aware of your "circle of faith" and that you are determined to stand in it as you read and study the Bible.

Let us examine the title of this book in order to guide ourselves in its development and fulfillment. A crucial distinction is being made between reading the Bible casually with curiosity and studying the Bible intensively as our primary written document and most important book in our lives. Five ways to read and to study the Bible are described on pages 15-19. There is certainly nothing wrong with reading the Bible as an adventure and for fun or in experiencing joy as we study the Bible seriously. However, studying the Bible as "the primal document" for ourselves and humankind is a most serious undertaking on a different level from reading and studying the Bible to satisfy our curiosity and to find entertainment. The title of this book includes all who read the Bible, for any reason, and especially those who study the Bible as their primary written document and most important road map through life. This guidebook strives to be inclusive and open to everyone, anywhere, anytime regardless of age, gender, race, religion and education. It is important for Christians to remember that the Bible belongs to all people since it proposes to describe all people and all things in relationship to God. The Bible is your Bible. Claim it!

The Bible indicated in the title is that collection of books well-known and recognized in classical Christianity and Western Civilization. In an Easter Letter dated A.D. 367, Athanasius listed for the first time the twenty-seven books which later became the New Testament. The sixty-six books of the Bible and the fourteen Apocryphal Books were identified, canonized and accepted by major churches in East and West as the sacred writings of Christendom in A.D. 397 at the Third Council of Carthage. Before A.D. 397, the churches simply had no identifiable book or collection of books or scrolls known as the Bible. The manuscripts which became the Bible existed and many of them were used by the churches and considered to be Holy Scripture. However, until A.D. 397, no collection of books or scrolls existed which one could hold in hand and say, "This book is the Bible." No collection of original manuscripts has been found and it is highly improbable that any original manuscripts still exist. Empirically, no original Bible as one book existed until the first Christian Bible was canonized in A.D. 397. Furthermore, if an original Bible existed, its meanings were not self-evident. The Bible is always subjectively interpreted. It is extremely important to know both what the Bible is and what the Bible is not. It is also crucial to know if claims made about the Bible are factual and have any historical connection to the Bible.

The Christian Bible includes the thirty-nine books of the Hebrew Bible and the twenty-seven books of the New Testament. As a Christian with deep roots in the Calvinistic and Free-Church traditions, I accept the conclusion in the 1647 Westminster Confession of Faith that the canon includes the thirty-nine books of the Old Testament and the twenty-seven books of the New Testament. The Bible has not been replaced in classical Christian traditions as the primal document for faith and practice by any other primary document(s) including narratives, creeds, confessions, edicts, theories, theologies, novels, inspirational books and individual opinions.

A Guidebook for Reading and Studying the Bible is a primer for learning the basics for reading and studying the Bible with faith, freedom, academic integrity, passion and confidence. One reason few helpful guidebooks are available is the incredible difficulty in writing one that is comprehensive, accurate, clear, relevant, understandable and appealing.

Individuals and small groups of Christians who find this book helpful can serve as their own instructors with one essential qualification. All who read and study the Bible need the guidance of God in interpreting the Bible and making it relevant. Christians usually speak of the guidance by God as the work of God the Holy Spirit for whom the norm of interpretation is the revelation of God in Jesus Christ (Jn. 14:25-26; 1 Jn. 4:1-3). Documents which became the Bible were spoken and written by men and women inspired by the Holy Spirit (2 Tim. 3:16-17; 2 Pet. 1:20-21). In A.D. 397, the Bible was canonized by leaders of the churches through the guidance of the Holy Spirit. The Bible is best interpreted by those inspired and enlightened by the Holy Spirit. For Christians, the Holy Spirit works with our minds and spirits enabling us to understand and to interpret the Bible in harmony with the revelation in Jesus Christ. As we read and study the Bible with teachable minds, open spirits and sincere hearts, the Holy Spirit guides our thinking and living in the ways which our Lord Jesus Christ thought and lived. With the Bible as our map and guide, we come in and go out and travel by faith where God is leading us in the kingdom of God, the churches and the world.

Reference has been made to "classical Christianity" which I interpret to mean the mainline Eastern Orthodox, Roman Catholic, Protestant, and Free-Church (not in a State-Church relationship) traditions which affirm, embrace and have not departed from the revelation in Jesus Christ as the norm of the Christian Faith with the Bible as the primal document for Christianity.

Christian education has failed primarily because disciples of Jesus Christ have given their responsibility for being educated in the Bible and the teachings of the Christian Faith to leaders of the churches. Christian ministers seldom give top priority to first-class educational programs for Christians. Jesus, The Teacher, gave first place in his ministry to the education of his Apostles and disciples. We have passively accepted what trickles down from others as true and all we need for genuine Christian education. The education of Christians will succeed to the extent that disciples of Jesus Christ accept responsibility for educating themselves in the best ways provided by the churches and in additional ways they can devise and implement. We must claim our freedom and responsibility for both believing in Jesus Christ and for superior Christian education. We need to be educated as to what the Gospel is, what it is not, and what it means to know the mind of Jesus Christ and the wisdom of the Holy Spirit. There is no substitute for being pro-active in studying the Bible and Christian tradition when the goal is excellence in Christian education.

Christians must be aggressive and responsible if Christian education is going to happen. Do not waste one hour of your precious time with ignorance and misinformation. The Bible never describes God the Father, God the Son, and God the Holy Spirit as ignorant or unlearned. Only false gods and idols are described in the Bible as ignorant. Willful ignorance is sinful and may be one of the most destructive and immoral of all sins. In civil law, ignorance of the law is no excuse. Christians who scoff at serious study of the Bible may exclaim, "Oh, I just take the Bible like it is!" This exclamation raises two very profound questions: "Which Bible?" and "How is it?"

Let us begin the engaging task of selecting and describing basic tools for reading and studying the Bible. Tools, however, are irrelevant if we do not actually read the Bible often, under many circumstances and with some plan for reading and studying the Bible. I usually read The Revised Standard Version (The Oxford Annotated Bible), The New American Standard Version, The Jerusalem Bible and The King James Version which was the Bible of my youth. The King James Version is, at times, still my favorite translation: e.g., the Twenty-Third Psalm, the Sermon on the Mount in Matthew, chapters 5-7, and Paul's chapter 13 on love in 1 Corinthians. Select one, or more, modern translations from Hebrew and Greek which seeks to give a literal translation when possible. Read a Bible with which you feel comfortable. Carry the Bible with you and with passion read and read again. God will guide you as you read and study the Bible and your life may be changed again and again, and often blessed, as you believe in and live out the Gospel! The Revised Standard Version is used in this book unless another translation is indicated.

II
EIGHT TOOLS
FOR STUDYING THE BIBLE

E very study project has its subject-matter, tools with which to work, a plan and examples of how to proceed. The subject-matter of the Bible is the writings of the Old Testament and the New Testament. The tools are those which are common to the study of any literary document with special attention to those tools and materials related to the history and study of the Bible. The first tool is a small collection of books. (Examples of how to proceed begin on page 22.)

A. Tool One:
A Small Collection of Books

Three books are essential in beginning a serious study of the Bible. First, it is important to choose a modern translation of the Bible which is as literal as possible in harmony with a good style. Select a translation which you prefer and enjoy. Second, a current edition of a dictionary such as *Webster's Collegiate Dictionary of the English Language* is essential. Third, a concordance is helpful for locating texts in the Bible. *Cruden's Complete Concordance* is easy to use.

Five additional books, or books like them, are exceedingly helpful. Recently revised editions may be preferable. First, *The Westminster Historical Atlas to the Bible* is an excellent source for the geography and history of the Bible and its environment in the context of world history. Second, *The New Westminster Dictionary of the Bible* includes helpful definitions and valuable materials such as an overview of each of the

7

sixty-six books of the Bible. Third, *The Westminster Dictionary of Christian Theology* provides often needed theological definitions and information. Fourth, a collection of biblical commentaries on specific books of the Bible or a complete series of commentaries may be very helpful. My favorite series is *The Interpreter's Bible*, twelve volumes. A new edition is currently being published by Abingdon Press. *The Interpreter's One-Volume Commentary on the Bible* is also excellent. Fifth, a survey of the history of the Bible and its development in Judaism and Christianity can be extremely informative and enlightening. *How We Got Our Bible* by T. C. Smith is accurate and reader friendly.

Several translations of the Bible in one volume can be extremely helpful in comparing texts. The Holy Bible in Four Translations, including The King James Version, is outstanding. The Layman's Parallel Bible has three translations and The Living Bible which is a paraphrase.

B. Tool Two:
Selection of a Norm

Tool number one is physical, like a hammer or a paint brush, and you can hold these books in your hands. The rest of the tools are mainly "thought tools" which we hold in our minds. God works through both physical tools and thought tools. The first thought tool is the norm you choose for reading, studying and interpreting the Bible. A norm is a standard for measuring and evaluating things and ideas. The metric system is a norm for measuring empirical data. The Myers-Briggs Type Indicator is a norm for measuring and evaluating types of personalities. Also, the Apostles' Creed is a norm for evaluating theological teachings, writings and making value judgments regarding orthodoxy and heresy. Confessions of faith are being used more often today by individual churches and denominations as "creeds" for the same purposes described above.

For Christians, the revelation in Jesus Christ is the norm for knowing all reality directly or indirectly. Although we may not be fully aware of it when we become Christians, this tool is automatically chosen when we become disciples of the Lord Jesus Christ. This norm is all-embracing since the God revealed in Jesus Christ is the God who creates and redeems all things, the God who is in heaven and on earth. For Christians the revelation in Jesus Christ is the normative revelation for all reality. It is necessary to be crystal clear in understanding that this is the norm for our lives in order that we may know when we are thinking and living in harmony with the Christian norm for faith and practice. Therefore, the selection of a norm is also your choice of the first and most important thought tool for reading and studying the Bible.

A Christian reads the Bible by relating all of the Bible, in one way or another, to what has been revealed to the Apostles and other disciples of Jesus as recorded in the New Testament. John 3: 16 describes Jesus Christ as the only and unique Son of God and indicates that his mission in the world is to give eternal life to believers. John 3:16 is one clear statement of the norm of the Christian Faith. Some additional statements of this norm are: Mk. 8:29; Mt. 16:16; Jn. 1:14; Acts 2:36; Rom. 10:9; 1 Cor. 2:2; Gal. 1:11-12; Eph. 1:9-10; Phil. 2:9-11; Col. 1:19-20; 2:9; Heb. 1:1–4; and Rev. 21:22-26. In classical Christianity the normative revelation is the life of Jesus, his ministry, teachings, gathering of Apostles and disciples, suffering, death, burial, descent into hell, resurrection, appearances, ascension and Pentecost (See article two of the Apostles' Creed).

Every major religion or philosophy is grounded in a norm which has been intentionally selected and often personally embraced. Judaism, Christianity and Islam select different norms although all or some parts of the Christian Bible function as primary written documents in these religions. The Hebrew Bible is what Christians know as the Old Testament including the Books of the Law, the Prophets and the Writings. The Hebrew Bible became the Bible of Judaism, officially, at the Council of Jamnia in A.D. 90. In A.D. 397, the major Christian churches accepted this identical Hebrew Bible without change (astounding indeed!) as a part of the Christian Bible. Some Jews choose Genesis 12:1-3; Exodus 3:13-17; 20:1-17 or Deuteronomy 6:4 to describe their normative revelation of God, Yahweh, in the Promise to Abraham, the Covenant of the Law given to Moses or the Shema. Then, they interpret all of the Hebrew Bible in relationship to this norm. The same analogy or procedure holds true for all major religions, philosophies and other comprehensive and responsible interpretations of reality. Another religious example is Mohammed whose life and teachings are the normative revelation of Allah for Islam as described in the Koran. For Islam, the norm is the revelation of Allah through Mohammed the prophet and his writings.

C. Tool Three:
A "Critical Principle" for Interpreting the Bible

The revelation in Jesus Christ is the Christian norm for reality. How is this norm to be used in interpreting redemption and creation revealed in Jesus Christ? There must be something within the norm for knowing the reality of the revelation through Jesus Christ, something which gives Christians a key (motif, theme, idea, concept) for a responsible and systematic interpretation of the Bible and the Christian Faith. That "something" is at the very heart of the norm, something which is a "critical principle" for interpreting the Bible.

Many answers have been given to the question of such a critical principle for interpreting the Bible and the Christian Faith: the holiness of God, the love of God, the grace of God, the justice of God, the righteousness of God, the sovereignty of God, the promise of God, the covenant of God, the law of God (ethics or morality), the kingdom of God, the church of God, knowledge of God, the Apostles' Creed, justification by faith, Christ and his benefits, our God-consciousness, the Word of God, the new being in Jesus as the Christ and, since the Reformation, certain theories about the Bible. Many of the critical principles listed above have been chosen by some outstanding theologians and ethicists in the history of Christianity. Among Protestant theologians some critical principles are well-known. Martin Luther chose justification by faith. Philip Melanchthon chose Christ and his benefits. John Calvin chose the sovereignty of God. Friedrich Schleiermacher chose human God-consciousness. Benjamin B. Warfield chose the plenary verbal theory of the inspiration of the Bible by the Holy Spirit. Paul Tillich chose the new being in Jesus as the Christ.

There is no perfect key to unlock the Bible or perfect critical principle to interpret the Bible, the Christian Faith and all reality. Some keys or critical principles appear to be more adequate and in harmony with the norm of the revelation in Jesus Christ than others. Often, we are not aware of the need for a critical principle. Therefore, at times we take with us different critical principles when we study the Bible. Little wonder that the study of the Bible is sometimes frustrating, fragmented and without a center. This is an opportunity for you to choose or reaffirm your critical principle for interpreting the Bible and the Christian Faith. My critical principle for interpreting the Bible, the Christian Faith and all reality is "the God who is love revealed in Jesus Christ" as described in the New Testament and interpreted in the context of the Old Testament.

D. Tool Four:
The Principle of the Closeness of Relationships

The "principle of the closeness of relationships" involves relevance. It is an inbuilt, innate ability grounded in human nature which functions both in involuntary and voluntary ways. We relate to the temperature of what is near us, hot or cold, first without thinking about it and then, if we are uncomfortable, by taking appropriate action. Everyone uses the principle of the closeness of relationships in all matters. The intentional or conscious use of this principle in reading and studying the Bible is crucial for our understanding the Bible and its relevance.

The following is an illustration of the relation of the principle of the closeness of relationships to the norm of the revelation in Jesus Christ. Two subjects: the suffering death of Jesus, on the one hand, and hairstyles, on the other, are chosen to illustrate this principle clearly.

For example, the passages in the Bible describing the suffering death of Jesus, though horrible and repulsive to some of us, cannot be ignored or relegated to a minor role in our interpretations of Jesus (Mk. 8:31; 14:65; 15:16-20, 25, 34-37; Jn. 19:1, 17-18; Acts 2:22-23; Rom. 5:6-8; 1 Cor. 1:22; 2:2; Gal. 2:20; Phil. 2:8; Heb. 5:7-10). Biblical passages describing hairstyles or haircuts are only somewhat relevant to the life of Jesus and the revelation of God. Thus, they are included as secondary in interpreting the biblical meaning of the revelation in Jesus Christ.

Although it may be assumed that Jesus wore his hair down to his shoulders, his hairstyle is not significant enough to be mentioned specifically in the New Testament. Other hairstyles are discussed in the Bible as significant in certain situations (2 Sam. 14:26; Jn. 11:2; 12:3; 1 Cor.

11:13–16; 1 Tim. 2:9; 1 Pet. 3:3). In fact, Mary's hairstyle is implied twice in relationship to her intimate act of drying the feet of Jesus with her long hair (Jn. 11:2; 12:3).

Between the suffering death of Jesus and hairstyles there is a great disparity in relationship to understanding the revelation in Jesus Christ. Mary's act of affection and concern for Jesus is evidence of an unusual kind of response made to Jesus. Also, the cultural and ethical practices of the time are reflected in terms of hairstyles in the Corinthian church (1 Cor. 11:13-16) and the Jerusalem church (1 Pet. 3:3). However, there appears to be no important connection between Absalom's unusually heavy hair (five pounds annually) and the revelation in Jesus Christ. This interesting information is actually of no significance when the principle of the closeness of relationships to the revelation in Jesus Christ is applied. Therefore, I would locate 2 Samuel 14:26 far, far away from the center of the circle of faith but not outside the circle since it is in the Bible and constitutes part of the background for a Christian interpretation of the revelation in Jesus Christ.

Using the principle of the closeness of relationships to the cross, which is Paul's favorite symbol for the Gospel message (1 Cor. 2:2), the subject of hairstyles would scarcely be included in a discussion of the person and work of Jesus Christ. In a discussion of ethics in the early church, hairstyles may appropriately be discussed. The point is that between the suffering death of Jesus and hairstyles there are many biblical passages of far greater significance to be interpreted in terms of the principle of the closeness of relationships of biblical passages to the revelation in Jesus Christ. This is one way, an example, of using some passages in studying the Bible and leaving others in the background. Jesus did not use all biblical passages in interpreting the Hebrew Bible.

Obviously, all serious study of the Bible by Christians involves an arrangement of biblical texts according to the norm of the revelation in Jesus Christ or some other norm. Everyone rearranges the Bible according to his or her norm, a critical principle and the principle of the closeness of relationships to the norm. This practice is often referred to as creating a canon within the canon of the Bible. Any minister who reviews the texts chosen for sermons over a few years can soon discover his or her norm, critical principle and principle of the closeness of relationships. The disclosure of a canon within the canon may be surprising and enlightening.

E. Tool Five:
The Relational Model

There appears to be within each of us a way of experiencing and interpreting all things in terms of relationships. Reality is not fictional. We have unique ways of viewing and arranging what is believed to exist. The result of this activity is frequently described as the formulation of his or her own world view. In all realms of human existence and in every academic discipline a relational model, of some kind, automatically comes into play. The pre-modern idea of substance as the essence of what is real has long since been questioned and largely replaced by relational models which lead to the conclusion that reality in itself is relational and consists of and in relationships.

The Christian revelation describes a new relational realism in which the norm is the revelation of all reality, directly or indirectly, in Jesus Christ as Lord in the kingdom of God and the kingdom of the world. The Bible is a collection of documents which describes some of these relationships, explicitly and implicitly, from the beginning to the end of history. A revelatory realism view of reality is mind-boggling! Since the rise of modern science, it has seldom been taken seriously and implemented in terms of the revelation of the God who is love revealed in Jesus Christ.

It is time for Christians and humankind to take the Bible seriously without ignoring or deifying it. This endeavor is too large and important to leave entirely to the churches and its leaders. The Bible is relevant not only to Jews, Christians and Muslims but to all humankind. It is the privilege and responsibility of every person to come to terms with the contents of the Bible using the norm and ultimate concern that each person embraces. The subject-matter of the Bible is God, creation, humankind and all other kind. The Bible itself is not the subject-matter and message of the Bible. For Christians, the Gospel of Jesus Christ is the central message in the Bible.

Six components of the relational model are essential in reading and studying the Bible from the perspective of the norm of revelation in Jesus Christ, a critical principle of interpretation and the principle of the closeness of relationships. The six components are: the God-God's Self relationship, the I-Self relationship, the I-God relationship, the I-Thee relationship, the I-You relationship and the I-It relationship. Actually, we begin consciously with the I-Self relationship in the midst of the last three relationships and proceed to the I-God relationship and the God-God's Self relationship. In this discussion, however, I begin with the God-God's Self relationship to illustrate the comprehensive context from which reality is perceived in and from the Christian circle of faith.

When a person has a good relationship to self, to God, to other selves in intimate relations, to other selves in casual relations and to creation, he or she experiences life as the fullness of what it can be and what it means to be fully human. Jesus in his humanity exhibits each of these relationships in the revelation of God. In Christian theology Jesus the Christ, the Son of God, is the norm for what it means to be fully human as well as the norm for what it means to be fully divine.

Therefore, as Christians, we begin with the circle of faith in which we stand, the norm of the revelation in Jesus Christ, a critical principle of interpretation and a relational model. Then, we come to the Bible, our primal document, to search for and describe the six components of the relational model as we know and experience them in Jesus Christ. The Bible describes these six components of the relational model in many literary forms such as: narrative, drama, myth, poetry, allegory, history, law, prophesy, proverb, apocalyptic image, gospel-narrative, parable, sermon, message, letter, biography, autobiography, commentary, theology, ethics and philosophy.

The relational model seems complicated because life is incredibly complex and multifaceted! We seldom find all six components of the relational model in one chapter in the Bible. In Colossians 1:1-29, however, these six components clearly emerge in Paul's classic description of the Lord Jesus Christ as the revelation of God. Here we behold an incredible description of the universality and particularity of all things in Jesus Christ. With our critical principle, we use the principle of the closeness of relationships to interpret these six components of the relational model.

Everything in the Bible, directly or indirectly, is described in terms of these six components of the relational model. This model clearly emerges from the revelation in the Lord Jesus Christ as a revelatory realism which is fully described in the Bible. The question, then, is how does the study of the Bible proceed in terms of these six relationships (Also, see pages 26-36).

1. The God-God's Self relationship
2. The I-Self relationship
3. The I-God relationship
4. The I-Thee relationship
5. The I-You relationship
6. The I-It relationship

F. Tool Six:
Eight Guidelines for Christians Who Study the Bible

1. The Bible as our primary written document
2. The texts of the Bible as generally agreed upon in the canon of sixty-six books
3. Inspiration of biblical writers by the Holy Spirit
4. The Bible as a unique and normative "faith-witness narrative"
5. The Holy Spirit as the divine partner in reading, studying and interpreting the Bible
6. The community of believers as partners in reading, studying and interpreting the Bible
7. Personal responsibility for reading, studying and interpreting the Bible
8. Reading and studying the Bible as an on-going, unfinished activity

G. Tool Seven:
Five Ways To Read and To Study the Bible

The contents of the Bible have been identified and affirmed. Six useful tools for studying the Bible have been described. It is time to discuss tool number seven, "five ways to read and to study the Bible." The following five ways may be helpful in setting your goal and designing your own plan to read and to study the Bible. You need a plan which best suits you, your decisions, goals and commitments while being in harmony with the revelation in Jesus Christ.

Five ways to read and to study the Bible are: browsing the Bible, devotional reading, public worship, small group study and intensive study.

These ways, at times, overlap and interpenetrate one another in your actual study of the Bible. Whether you read and study the Bible in one or more of these ways is your decision which is neither right nor wrong but a personal choice. In other words, you are not making a commitment to work from the first way through the fifth way unless this is your choice. Therefore, you do not necessarily fail if you never read the Bible in public worship or study the Bible intensively. Furthermore, this guidebook may have tremendous value for you even if you do not understand all of these five ways, or other parts of the book, when you read them the first or second time. You do not need to understand all of this guidebook in order to understand and to use some of it in remarkably helpful ways.

1. First Way: Browsing the Bible

Browsing the Bible is an excellent approach. It can be fun! We may call this a cursory way of reading the Bible. It may be described as an exploratory or investigative reading which is exciting, surprising and often opens up many hidden delights and possibilities. Recently, I was browsing the Bible and I read 1 John 4:7-21. In verses 8 and 16, I read "God is love" (Gk. *ho theos agape estin*). Reading these verses led me to read all of 1 John, 2 John and 3 John. Browsing the Bible led me to two other ways to read the Bible—devotional reading and intensive study—though I had not planned to go beyond just browsing the Bible.

Reading the Bible may become infectious and contagious. Once you begin, you may develop a passion for it and enter a new, sometimes strange, dangerous, fascinating and enchanting world. Studying the Bible is like learning about the pearl of great price, the unfolding of mysterious stories with many endings and no final ending in sight. You may experience the thrill of venturing into the wilderness of existence, the abyss of life and death, being and non-being, the ocean and the mountains, the garden of love, sin, and grace and the kingdom of God in the Lord Jesus Christ.

2. Second Way: Devotional Reading

Devotional Reading is important in improving your spiritual life and equipping you for living each day with an awareness of the loving and secure presence of God no matter what happens during that day. My day often begins with praying the Lord's Prayer, singing the Doxology and

Gloria Patri and reciting the Apostles' Creed. I usually read from one of the Gospels, Psalms or Proverbs. In meditation, I become keenly aware that I am a being-redeemed citizen in the kingdom of God. I am reminded of the divine and human resources available for my daily agenda.

The central message in the New Testament is the Gospel, Good News, of Jesus Christ in whom the kingdom of God is ushered into history (Mk. 1:14-15). Being aware that I am in the kingdom of God puts me in a frame of mind in which I am not bound to the kingdom of this world. In the New Testament, the kingdom of this world is the realm where evil and sin are exhibited and where God is not truly known, loved and served. Living in the kingdom of God is not an escape from the world but a victory over the power of the kingdom of this world. Reality for me is the kingdom of the God who is love and who invites everyone to enter into and to dwell in this kingdom while still living in the kingdom of the world. Being a liberated citizen in the kingdom of God's love in Jesus Christ gives me much courage, hope and assurance for the day. My day often ends with readings from the Psalms and the Epistles and offering prayers for others with gratitude and thanksgiving for my citizenship in God's kingdom and commonwealth.

We may decide to supplement our devotional readings in the Bible by reading other devotional materials. It is important to remember that devotional books are not the Bible. Inevitably, these writings promote in some ways the authors' plans, goals and agendas. When we use other devotional materials, we must not neglect the Bible and we must be quick to remember that for Christians the Bible is our primary book for devotion, meditation and spiritual growth.

3. Third Way: Public Worship

Reading the Bible is an extremely important medium of public worship. In many congregations, reading the Bible in public worship takes the forms of reading in unison, responsive readings, readings from the lectionary and readings by worship leaders. Until the Fifteenth Century, most Christians had no general access to the Bible. They participated in public reading of the Bible as passive listeners rather than readers. The priests had primary access to the Bible and they often hindered Christians from free access to the Bible in order to maintain the church's authority and

control by keeping people largely ignorant of the Bible. Johann Guten-
burg's invention of the printing press around A.D.1448 soon gave most
Christians freedom to read the Bible without obtaining permission from
the churches and without being supervised by ecclesiastical authorities.
Congregational reading of the Bible in public worship is still not encouraged by some ministers and churches today.

Effective reading of the Bible in public worship by ministers and
others requires preparation, dedication and prayer. Sadly, we are often
content to listen to others read and interpret the Bible for us and to instruct
us concerning the will of God for our lives. For Christians public worship
of God includes congregational readings from the Bible and lectionaries
related to the revelation of God in Jesus Christ in the context of the entire
Bible.

4. Fourth Way: Small Group Study of the Bible

Since Christian churches developed as described by Luke in the Acts
of the Apostles, Christians have routinely gathered in small groups to
engage in biblical studies and to worship God. The earliest Christians first
studied the Hebrew Bible and the Septuagint and later the writings which
became the New Testament in A.D. 397. Jesus saw opportunities for his
disciples when they gathered in small groups as described in Matthew
when he said, "For where two or three are gathered in my name, there am
I in the midst of them" (Mt. 18:20). Unfortunately, gathering in small
groups not under supervision by leaders of the institutional churches has
not always been encouraged. However, this way of structuring reading and
studying the Bible has superb possibilities for first-rate education of
Christians not only in the Bible but in all phases of the Christian life and
fellowship. Christian education is far too important to leave entirely in the
hands of the leaders of Christian institutions including churches, denominations, seminaries and divinity schools.

The key to successful small group study of the Bible is shared leader-
ship and responsibility where participants feel free to study without fear,
without being labeled and without being dominated by any member of the
group. There are unique advantages in small group study. It can be mobile,
efficient, inexpensive, flexible, inspirational, intimate, challenging, fulfilling and open to the fellowship of learning and teaching in the churches, in

the workplaces and in the play-places of the world. As disciples of Jesus Christ, we are authorized to gather in his name for any purpose in harmony with the revelation of God in Jesus of Nazareth. Christians should feel free to organize groups to read and to study the Bible, remembering that the Holy Spirit's guidance is essential to the most beneficial study and that the church is wherever Christians gather.

5. Fifth Way: Intensive Study of the Bible

Intensive study of the Bible is for those who desire it with a passion. Therefore, it may or may not be for you. This does not mean you are disqualified from reading and studying the Bible in other ways. Intensive study of the Bible means to engage in a comprehensive, long-term study project with the goal of becoming knowledgeable of the Bible, its history, its place in the kingdom of God, the churches, the Christian life and the world. The goal is to become a capable interpreter of the Bible. An intensive study of the Bible involves commitment, focused mental activity, a teachable mind, a positive attitude, openness to new and different information and ideas, willingness to be guided by the Holy Spirit and a desire to run the risk of being challenged and changed.

H. Tool Eight:
A Plan for Reading and Studying the Bible

My suggested plan is for beginners to begin the study of the New Testament with a passage from the Gospel of Mark as presented on pages 36-43. Mark begins his narrative with the ministry of John the Baptist and the call and baptism of Jesus. In Mark 1:15, Jesus proclaims the theme of his messianic ministry which is the kingdom of God. Mark is probably the first and oldest Gospel (ca. A.D. 70) and it becomes the major source for the later and larger narratives presented by Luke and Matthew. Scholars speak hypothetically of this common part of the text in these three Gospels as the "Q" document (meaning "source" in the German word *quelle*) which is a unique source and may be the oldest available account of the teachings and ministry of Jesus.

Then, you can continue your study with the Gospel of Luke and the Acts of the Apostles. Luke and Acts present the earliest chronological overview of the history of the life of Jesus and the beginnings and expansion of the early church from Luke's perspective (Lk. 1:1-4; Acts 1:1). This overview helps to set the geographical, historical and cultural benchmarks for a study of the New Testament. Then, study Matthew for two reasons. First, Matthew is comprehensive like Luke (from birth narratives to the resurrection) and it is written from a more Jewish perspective. Luke was a Gentile. Second, Matthew, Mark and Luke are often called the "synoptic Gospels" due to their similar perspectives about the message and mission of Jesus and the chronology of the historical ministry of Jesus of Nazareth.

Then, study the Gospel of John with its Hellenistic (Greek) perspective which varies considerably in structure, content, scope, history, theology and culture from Mark, Matthew and Luke. Continue with 1, 2 and 3 John for a cross-sectional look at the early Hellenistic church, its life, theology and ethics near the end of the first Christian Century.

Paul's writings are earlier than the synoptic Gospels, the Gospel of John and Letters of John. The Letters of Paul exhibit both the Judaic and also some Hellenistic perspectives and influences. Begin your study of the writings of Paul with 1 and 2 Thessalonians (Paul's earliest letters ca. A.D. 44-46) and continue with Romans, Galatians, 1 and 2 Corinthians, Ephesians, Philippians, Colossians, 1 and 2 Timothy, Titus and Philemon. Then, study the General Epistles: Hebrews, 1 and 2 Peter, James and Jude. Study Revelation later since it is apocalyptic and very complex.

My suggested plan is to study the Old Testament along with the study of the New Testament since they are intertwined and the study of one often greatly enriches the other and discloses the intimacies of their relationships. In the Old Testament begin with the Books of Law and History: Genesis, Exodus, Leviticus, Numbers, Deuteronomy, Joshua, Judges, Ruth, 1 and 2 Samuel, 1 and 2 Kings, 1 and 2 Chronicles, Ezra, Nehemiah and Esther. Then, study the Major and Minor Prophets: Isaiah, Jeremiah, Lamentations, Ezekiel, Daniel, Hosea, Joel, Amos, Obadiah, Jonah, Micah, Nahum, Habakkuk, Zephaniah, Haggai, Zechariah and Malachi. Continue with your study of the Writings: Job, Psalms, Proverbs, Ecclesiastes and Song of Solomon. A good plan is to read the prophets and other relevant books in the context of their historical periods. Obviously, browsing the Bible, devotional reading and reading the Bible in private and public worship will follow different sequences from that given above for intensive study in small or large groups.

Perhaps you have noticed that I make a distinction between the Hebrews and the Jews based on the period before the Exile to Babylon and after the return to Jerusalem. The Hebrew people began with Abraham (Gen. 12:1-3) around 2,000 B.C. and they were radically changed during and after the Exile (587-538 B.C.). After the Exile, Mordecai is identified as a Jew in the Old Testament (Esther 2:5; 3:4; 6:10, 13; 10:3). Other references to Jews do not identify individuals by name. Judaism emerges out of the Hebrew Faith but it is different in several important ways.

Give yourself great flexibility in reordering the sequence of the books you study and do not take my suggestions as necessarily best for you. In time you will figure out the best sequence for your studies. You will soon discover that there are favorite books of the Bible to which you turn almost automatically. A canon within the canon will begin to emerge and you must be very careful not to ignore other parts of the Bible.

It is crucial to remember that the Bible is a unique means of knowing the God revealed in Jesus Christ, but the Bible itself is not divine and does not make that claim for itself. According to Martin Luther, the Bible is the cradle in which the Christ child is laid. Care should be taken not to fall into the trap of worshiping the Bible instead of the God revealed through the Bible. When a theory about the Bible becomes the norm and the critical principle for studying the Bible, Jesus Christ is replaced as the norm and the result is a sect or a different religion. When the Bible is exalted to a divine status, many Christians and Christian leaders remain largely ignorant of and blind to the meaning of the Bible and the revelation of God in Jesus Christ. It is ironic and tragic that since Benjamin B. Warfield (1851-1921), the Bible has become for many Christians and churches the greatest barrier to the study of the Bible. For a critique and analysis of Warfield's view of the Bible, see *The Uses of Scripture In Recent Theology* (pages 17-24) by David H. Kelsey (1975).

III
HOW TO PROCEED IN READING
AND STUDYING THE BIBLE

───────────⫷◦◦◦⫸───────────

Remember, the most difficult step in any journey is the first one. There is in many of us a self-protective, stubborn resistance to beginning a demanding, difficult and threatening project. Only a burning passion for the project will set us free to make a commitment to it. You must deal with this matter if you intend to engage in intensive study of the Bible. Let readers begin by selecting their tools for studying the Bible. It is important for you to take your notebook seriously and put in writing what you are thinking and how you are proceeding in learning to study the Bible.

A. Gather Your Tools:
Tool One through Tool Seven

1. Tool One

Read again, Tool One: A Small Collection of Books (p. 7). If you followed suggestions regarding the first three books for your collection, then purchase as your fourth and fifth books, *The Westminster Historical Atlas of the Bible* and *How We Got Our Bible*. Make plans for getting other books recommended as you see the need for them. Of course, the internet is also an excellent reference source for biblical studies. Your next six tools are primarily "thought tools" which you also select. Record these books and your thought tools in your notebook.

2. Tool Two

Read again, Tool Two: Selection of a Norm (pp. 8-10). First, understand clearly the meaning and significance of a norm. The choice of a norm is the most important decision you make in studying the Bible. Then, choose or reaffirm your norm for interpreting the Bible. Since Pentecost, the norm in classical Christianity has been "the revelation of God in Jesus Christ." This is often called the "Christological norm." You can accept this norm as simply stated here or modify it to suit yourself. Remember, if the revelation in Jesus Christ is not your norm, you have probably departed from an authentic Christian norm and have adopted a Christian sect and/or a different religion. Record your norm in your workbook for reaffirmation, review and possible revision.

3. Tool Three

Read again, Tool Three: A "Critical Principle" for Interpreting the Bible (pp. 10-11). The selection of a critical principle for interpreting the Bible is your second most important decision. It must be in harmony with the norm of the revelation of God in Jesus Christ. It must be central and related to the views of God in the Bible. It must be clear and capable of being related, directly or indirectly, to all biblical passages and to all reality. My critical principle for interpreting the Bible and all reality is "the God who is love revealed in Jesus Christ" (p. 11). The following are a few passages which describe the centrality of the love of God and the essence of God's own being as love: Jn. 3:16; 1 Jn. 4:8, 16; Mk. 2:28-34; Dt. 6:4; 7:6-11; Rom. 5:8; and 1 Cor. 13:1-13.

"God is love" is the center of the primal analogy for all reality. The God who is love is the center of the circle in which Jesus Christ stands and which becomes our circle of faith. There is no other analogy by which this primal analogy of love can be interpreted. The mystery which inheres in this analogy transcends human reason including our capacity for analysis and comprehension. Furthermore, this indwelling mystery of the God who is love is both hidden and revealed in Jesus Christ. The mystery of love is best mediated through ways, media, which are in harmony with love itself so that these media become transparent to the presence of love, that is, the presence of God. To experience God's presence daily is the essence of peace and well-being (Heb. *shalom*, peace). For the Apostles and other disciples, Jesus became transparent to the presence of God who is love and who loves humankind and all living beings and things. Jesus Christ also becomes transparent to the presence of God in our midst through the work of the Holy Spirit.

4. Tool Four

Read again, Tool Four: The Principle of the Closeness of Relationships (pp. 11-13). Although this tool is commonplace, it must be used with great care in determining which biblical passages are of more or less importance in an adequate Christian interpretation of the Bible. No one has ever actually used all passages in the Bible as of equal importance. The example of Jesus is our criterion as we observe his selective use of the principle of closeness of relationships of the Hebrew Scriptures to him and his messianic ministry. Some biblical passages are simply more important and relevant than others. We learn many things about our theological views when we compare and contrast the biblical passages we use with the biblical passages we do not use.

The illustration given on pages 11-13 shows how the principle of the closeness of relationships functions in biblical studies and interpretation. It is the privilege and responsibility of each Christian to decide how close to the center of the circle (Jesus Christ) each biblical passage should be interpreted and whether the passage is close enough to have any direct part in understanding the revelation of God in Jesus Christ and the Christian life. As you begin to understand the principle of the closeness of relationships of passages in the Bible to the revelation in the Lord Jesus Christ, record in your notebook your understanding with an example of how this principle works.

The forms of a servant, servant forms, are primary but not exclusive in the mediation of love. In my earlier development of a systematic theology, I spoke of "love in the form of the Servant Jesus Christ" as my critical principle. Of course, love in the form of the Servant Jesus Christ is central but it is also too restrictive. Jesus said, "No longer do I call you servants, for the servant does not know what his master is doing; but I have called you friends, for all I have heard from my Father I have made known to you" (Jn. 15:15). Now, my critical principle is "the God who is love revealed in Jesus Christ." God is best known through the ways, media, of love revealed in Jesus Christ the norm of the Christian Faith (1 Cor. 13:1-13). God is also revealed through media other than the forms of a servant and these revelations are to be interpreted by Christians in terms of their closeness of relationships to the revelation in Jesus Christ. The media of love are those words and multiple forms of reality most transparent to the redeeming presence and glory of God. The incarnation of God in Jesus of Nazareth is the normative medium of love for Christians.

5. Tool Five

Read again, Tool Five: The Relational Model (pp. 13-15). Remember, these are the six relationships we see in the Bible as they have to do with the God who is love revealed in Jesus Christ, creation, history and the human conscience. These relationships emerge as we study the Bible but they do not appear in any systematic order since they are described primarily in narratives and also in other literary forms such as the parables of Jesus, apocalyptic images and poetry. It is our responsibility to interpret these relationships in terms of the norm of revelation in Jesus Christ.

6. Tool Six

Read again, Tool Six: Eight Guidelines for Christians Who Study the Bible (p. 15). It is your opportunity and responsibility to affirm and to list in your notebook your guidelines for reading and studying the Bible. Make certain that your guidelines do not take away the significance of the norm of revelation in Jesus Christ and the primacy of the Bible over tradition in matters of faith and practice, that is, doctrine and ethics. These guidelines are extremely influential in forming and shaping the tools for studying the Bible.

7. Tool Seven

Read again, Tool Seven: Five Ways To Read and To Study the Bible (pp. 15-19). You have arrived at the place where you are now beginning to decide "how you are going about" reading and studying the Bible. Select the tools and continue to write in your notebook your plan for reading and studying the Bible. The topical and expository methods are two primary examples of how the Bible has been read and studied with great success by Christians and others (pp. 26-43).

B. Make Your Plan:
Tool Eight

Preparing for reading and studying the Bible is perhaps a much longer and more complex project than you anticipated. You have come to the place where your hard work begins blessing you with enjoyable benefits. Unlike many Christians who go through the motions of reading and studying the Bible for decades, or a lifetime, and end with frustration and emptiness, you are now ready to tailor-make your own plan. Everything you have decided about the tools is now a part of your plan for reading and studying the Bible. The plan itself emerges as your major tool and master blueprint. Describe the plan in an easy to understand summary and use your plan to proceed step by step in your study of the Bible. Your plan is a continuing project throughout your life.

Review your new plan and make certain it is crystal clear, that you have included all essential components, and that you are able to accept it and make a commitment to it so that you can implement it with passion. Be patient and pace yourself as you make and remake your plan for reading and studying the Bible. This is a sizable project with many new ideas and tools. One of the best ways to study the Bible is with a small group of Christians, two to seven, who make a commitment to God, themselves and to one another to read and to study the Bible.

C. The Relational Model:

As we consider the topical and expository methods for studying the Bible, it is essential to understand the "The Relational Model" shown on page 27. This model is discussed thoroughly on pages 13-15. Then, the relational model is "put into practice" in the study of God using the topical method (pp. 26-36) and the study of Mark 12:28-34 employing the expository method (pp. 26-36). The Relational Model (p. 27) involves all reality, directly or indirectly, and it presents a "world view" from a Christian perspective.

D. The Topical Method for Studying the Bible

1. A Description of the Topical Method

The topical method for reading and studying the Bible is exceedingly popular. It is used in browsing the Bible, devotional reading, public wor-

The Relational Model

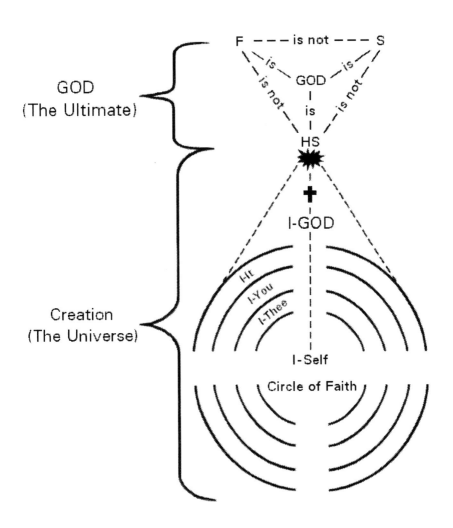

ship, small group study and intensive study of the Bible. The use of a concordance to locate desired words and topics is helpful and saves time. Christian ministers in churches and in other institutions of Christianity, scholars in many disciplines and practitioners and politicians of every sort are adept in using the topical method for reading and studying the Bible. My example for the topical method is to study "God" who is the primary subject or topic in the Bible. We begin the topical method with the study of biblical passages which describe the God of the Bible. Our first task is to identify tools for this study.

Four tools are especially helpful in the study of this topic. They are a norm, a critical principle, a principle of the closeness of relationships and a relational model. The norm is the revelation of God in Jesus Christ. God is interpreted in relationship to this norm. The critical principle is the revelation of the God who is love. The principle of the closeness of relationships of Jesus to God is described thoroughly in the New Testament, especially in the Father and Son relationship. We select biblical passages connected to the God of the Hebrews, Jews and Jesus of Nazareth. Then, God is interpreted in terms of the six components of the relational model as these are described in the Bible as the revelation of the God who is love revealed through Jesus Christ.

The second task is to study the context of each passage adequately to avoid an interpretation of the passage which is out of harmony with its context. At this point, it is imperative that we learn the type of literature we are studying. For example, studying poetic literature as if it is scientific information creates all kinds of problems. Failure to identify accurately the type of literature being studied is a disastrous mistake in studying the Bible. Knowing the context enables us to avoid eisegesis which means a faulty or spurious interpretation of the passage by reading into the text our own ideas. Performing this second task enables us to avoid setting forth a "patchwork" view of God configured by our own ideas of God with biblical proof-texts.

The third task is to present our study of God, or any topic, as a work in progress rather than a finished project which is the absolute truth and, therefore, must not be revised. Our study of God is brief. A definitive and fully developed view of God is long and complex. A comprehensive study of God will be found in any adequate book in Christian systematic theology or dogmatics (See Emil Brunner's *Dogmatics*, vol. 1 and Paul Tillich's *Systematic Theology*, vols. 1 and 3).

2. The Topical Method and the Study of God

The subjects of the Bible appear in this order: God, creation and humankind. Our tendency is to see ourselves as the primary subject in the Bible. The biblical narrative describes God as being involved with men and women of faith and unbelief as they describe in writing their stories of good and evil, sin and grace, and love and hate in the drama of creation and redemption.

God is described in many ways in the Bible which do not easily fit together. Who is this God revealed in Jesus Christ? John writes, "And the Word was made flesh and dwelt among us, full of grace and truth; we have beheld his glory, glory as of the only Son from the Father" (Jn. 1:14). Paul writes, "That is, God was in Christ, reconciling the world to himself" (2 Cor. 5:19a). In Colossians, Paul writes, "For in him all the fulness of God was pleased to dwell" (Col. 1:19) and "For in him the whole fulness of deity dwells bodily" (Col. 2:9). Jesus says, "He who has seen me has seen the Father" (Jn. 14:9b) and in John 17:22, Jesus in prayer says to the Father, "The glory which thou has given me I have given to them, that they may be one even as we are one."

The Christian message centers on the "revelation of God" in Jesus Christ. Again, which God is revealed in Jesus Christ? Here is where the critical principle (third tool) comes into action in searching the Bible for the God revealed in Jesus Christ. On pages 10-11, I stated my critical principle as "the God who is love revealed in Jesus Christ." We apply the critical principle using the principle of the closeness of relationships (fourth tool) to describe the components of the relational model (fifth tool). The New Testament describes God and Jesus Christ in the relational model as the God who is love in six relationships: the God-God's Self, I-Self, I-God, I-Thee, I-You and I-It relationships. [See *I and Thou* (1937) by Martin Buber, *Truth as Encounter* (1943) by Emil Brunner, *Personal Knowledge* (1958) by Michael Polanyi, *The Secular City* (1965) and *Religion and the Secular City* (1984) by Harvey Cox for discussions of some of these six relationships.]

3. The Topical Method: God and the Relational Model

The center of our circle of faith is the revelation in Jesus Christ and in this center Jesus Christ becomes transparent to the God who is love (1 Jn. 4:8, 16). From the center, the creation is thus revealed to be the work of God and the object of God's redeeming love (Jn. 3:16; Rom. 8:19-23; Rev. 21:1-4; Gen. 1:31; Ps. 8:3-8; 19:1-6). Humankind comes into the biblical accounts as a part of creation, the crown of creation (Gen. 1:26-31; 2:4b-25; Deut. 7:6-8; Ps. 8:3-8; Mt. 6:26; Mk.2:27), the tragedy of creation (Gen. 3:1-24; 6:5-7; Jn. 2:24-25; Rom. 3:23) and the object of God's redemptive love (Jn. 3:16; Rom. 5:8; 2 Cor. 5:17; 1 Jn. 4:9-10) in forgiveness (Mk. 11:25; Lk. 23:34; 1 Jn. 1:9), reconciliation (2 Cor.5:18-19) and recapitulation (Eph. 1:10).

Notice the negative responses to the God who is love. They are dealt with in the death and resurrection of Jesus. John writes, "He who commits sin is of the devil; for the devil has sinned from the beginning. The reason the Son of God appeared was to destroy the works of the devil" (1 Jn. 3:8). Sin and evil are inescapable topics in the center of the revelation of God in Jesus Christ. The Bible describes the ecstacy and the agony, the continuing hope and tragedy, the fallen creation and the redemption of all creation in narratives spanning two thousand years.

At this point we turn to the relational model to illustrate some of what the Bible describes about these relationships. Each of these six relationships is described in biblical passages related to God. These six relationships involve mysteries at the core of all reality. Authentic mysteries can be experienced and described, more or less adequately, but they cannot be fully explained or demonstrated. It is presumptuous to attempt a full and complete explanation of the mystery of God or to offer absolute proofs for the existence of God. God is known by faith (Heb. 11:6).

a. The God-God's Self Relationship

The description of the God-God's Self relationship in no way seeks to be definitive. With our tools and plan, we proceed to show that in the Bible God is described and affirmed as love (Gk. *agape*, unqualified affection for the other). We read in 1 John 4:8, "He who does not love does not know God; 'for God is love'" (Gk. *hoti o theos agape estin*). And in 1 John 4:16, "So we know and believe the love

God has for us. 'God is love' (Gk. *ho theos agape estin*), and he who abides in love abides in God, and God abides in him." One helpful way to describe the Trinity is to say something like: "God the Father loves God the Son in God the Holy Spirit; God the Son loves God the Father in God the Holy Spirit; and God the Holy Spirit loves God the Father and God the Son in their love for one another." This relational love in the God-God's Self relationship is the ontological basis for all reality and for knowledge of God and all other things, that is, for knowing what is to be known. This is an ontology (Gk. *ontos*, being + *logos*, word) and an epistemology (Gk. *episteme*, knowledge + *logos*, word) rooted in faith. This is a theory of being and knowing. A function of reason is to describe faith-knowledge but not to explain it. All knowing presupposes and believes there is something to know and that in part we can know it.

God the Father's response at the baptism of Jesus is, "Thou art my beloved Son; with thee I am well pleased" (Mk. 1:11b) and at the transfiguration, "This is my beloved Son, listen to him" (Mk. 9:7b). Jesus says to his disciples, "As the Father has loved me, so have I loved you; abide in my love" (Jn. 15:9). Jesus speaks again of the Father's love for him (Jn. 17:23, 26) and also of the eternal presence of the Father's love with him, "Father, I desire that they also, whom thou hast given me, may be with me where I am, to behold my glory which thou hast given me in thy love for me before the foundation of the world" (Jn. 17:24). The Trinity is the Christian doctrine of God, developed ca. A.D. 150-451, based on the revelation of God in Jesus Christ. The revelation of God who is love in Jesus Christ is the norm for our knowing the God-God's Self relationships.

b. The I-Self Relationship

Actually, we always begin with ourselves and the relationships we have to ourselves. From birth to death, we are dealing with ourselves one way or another every moment of our existence. Little wonder that we are preoccupied with ourselves since it is impossible to escape from ourselves entirely. We may become preoccupied with (in love with) other persons and things which make the self secondary for a brief period of time. However, we always return to ourselves and our

I-Self relationship. From Genesis 1:26-31 to Revelation 22:21, every narrative, every biography and every autobiography in the Bible deals in some way with the I-Self relationship. What does the Bible describe about the God who is love and our human I-Self relationship?

Since Jesus is our norm and Jesus is fully human, what does the Bible say about the relationship which Jesus has to himself? Perhaps the earliest evidence of the I-Self relation in Jesus becomes apparent when he is twelve years of age and in the Temple in Jerusalem (Lk. 2:41-52). Mary and Joseph are astonished at his insensitivity to them by remaining in Jerusalem without informing them. "And he said to them, 'How is it that you sought me? Did you not know that I must be in my Father's house?' And they did not understand the saying which he spoke to them" (Lk. 2:49-50). Jesus was aware of a relationship to himself which caused him to interpret being in his Father's house as more important than telling his parents his whereabouts. How does Jesus understand himself? The synoptic Gospels present him as a man who is constantly dealing with who he is and his mission in life. Scholars describe his quest in the Gospel narratives as Jesus and his messianic consciousness. Jesus probably did not know the full meaning of his messiahship until his I-Self relationship was fully disclosed in the Garden of Gethsemane (Mk. 14:32-42). Like Jesus, each of us deals with his or her own humanity, I-Self relationship, and self-identity and we are constantly interpreting its meaning until we die. Jesus is the norm for our I-Self relationships.

So what do we do with the I-Self relationship to God who is love and loves us? We follow the example of Jesus in truly seeking an authentic I-Self relationship in the midst of the love of God. Jesus says, "But seek ye first the kingdom of God, and his righteousness; and all these things shall be added unto you" (Mt. 6:33, KJV). God's kingdom is the redemptive realm of God's love.

c. The I-God Relationship

God is that reality to which we actually give our first loyalty or ultimate concern (Paul Tillich), our number one priority in daily activities. To describe the I-God relationship, we must do some serious thinking about who is our God. This is exactly what Jesus does and then he decides to be baptized by John the Baptist (Mk 1:9-11). Immediately, Jesus goes into the wilderness to think about what this commitment in baptism means. The answer comes in his temptations to choose another option than the God into whose name he was baptized (Mk. 1:12-13; Lk. 4:1-13; Mt. 4:1-11). Jesus struggles with his options and finally reaffirms his choice of the God of his baptism. Our striving for God and the kingdom of God is constantly encouraged by the experience of God's love in Jesus Christ and our own experience that God is love (Jn. 3:16, 1 Jn. 4:16). Thus, Jesus is our norm for knowing God and how to relate to God in our I-God relationships.

In the I-Thee, I-You, and I-It relationships, the God who is love is revealed in Jesus Christ and described in relation to responses to God's love by Jesus and by all who love God with all the heart, soul, mind, and strength and the neighbor as the self (Dt. 6:4; Lev. 19:18b; Mk. 12:29-31). Humankind and all creation are always involved with the God who loves and reveals God's Self (Is. 2:4; 9:1-7; 11:6-9; 40:12-31; Jer. 31:31-34; Jn. 10:16; Eph. 4:4-6; 1 Pet. 2:9-10; Mic.4:5).

d. The I-Thee Relationship

The I-Thee relationship describes a person in intimate, in-depth, and fulfilling experiences with another person. These precious relationships, in which we are soul-mates, are often associated with family, marriage, friends, colleagues, and infrequent but soul-stirring and life-shaping encounters with strangers. Jesus exhibits I-Thee relationships with God the Father, God the Holy Spirit, Mary, Joseph, his six or more brothers and sisters, John the Baptist, his Apostles and some other disciples, especially a few like Mary Magdalene, Mary, Martha and Lazarus. Jesus is open to I-Thee relationships and connections to all with whom he comes in contact (Mk. 14:35-36; 6:3, 7-13; Mt. 1:18-25; Lk. 7:28; 23:42-43; 24:10-11; Jn. 11:1-44). The revelation of the God who is love in Jesus Christ is the norm for our I-Thee relationships.

e. The I-You Relationship

The I-You relationship is not less personal, in intention, than the I-Thee relationship. But it is less intimate since it is impossible for any person to have intimate relationships with all humans encountered. The I-You relationship is both individual and corporate or societal. It is based on the fact that all humans are created equal and treated with equal regard and respect by God who creates all men and women in the image of God (Gen. 1:26-27; 5:1-2; 9:6). Jesus treats all humans with equal respect and dignity. He does not treat some of their words and deeds with respect (Mt. 23:1-39). He regards all humans as made in the image of God and those for whom he is to die (Lk. 23:34; Rom. 8:29; 1 Cor. 15:49; 2 Cor. 3:18; 4:4; Col. 1:15; 3:10; Heb. 1:3). The revelation of the God who is love in Jesus Christ is the norm for our I-You relationships.

f. The I-It Relationship

We are often unaware that we are essentially related to creation (nature) until we feel sharp pain, become ill, grow older and approach death. The first humans tended to worship the sun, moon, stars, earth and water as their faith responded to what was offered them. We tend to make a different response by relating to creation as an enemy to be controlled, managed, exploited and conquered. Relationships to all things created (the It world) can be seen in terms of the norm of the revelation of the God who is love in Jesus Christ. The boundaries between the It world and the Self world overlap and interpenetrate one another. These boundaries are not easy to identify.

Jesus understands creation as God's gracious work in itself and for itself and he describes it as a field and a garden for humankind's well-being and joy (Gen. 1:26-31; Mt. 6:26-33). The Son of God participates in the beginning of all creation (Jn. 1:1, 10; Col. 1:15-17; Heb. 1:1-2). When Jesus the Son of God dies, the creation cannot be silent (Mt. 27:45, 51-54) since it is also being crucified. The creation itself is to be renewed and transformed into a new creation at the end of the present age (Rom. 8:18-23; 1 Cor. 15:42-50; Eph. 1:9-10; Col. 1:18-20; Rev. 21:1-4). Again, the revelation of the God who is love in Jesus Christ is the norm for our I-It relationships.

God seeks and communicates with all people and all things. This is *theosynpanism* (Gk. *theos*, God + *syn*, in, under, with + *pan*, all things): God in, under, with and through all things (Eph. 4:46; Rom. 11:36; 1 Cor. 8:6; Col. 1:15-19; Heb. 2:10; Acts 17:28). Also, this view may be called *pansyntheism*: All things in, under, with and through God. This view is in harmony with the relational model of reality in both theology and science. Love (*agape*) in some form is the "glue" which holds all things together and inheres in the very being of God. In *The Elegant Universe*, Dr. Brian Greene describes a similar phenomenon from a scientific perspective as a "super-string theory" (pp. x., 13-17, 345-87) in his quest for an ultimate theory of everything. He does not deal with philosophy of science, philosophy or theology but he automatically enters these disciplines as he writes in terms of the "ultimate" and "everything." Cosmology and cosmogony then involve ontology (metaphysics). Greene does not discuss ontology or metaphysics per se in his book.

In conclusion, God is also described in the Bible in a multitude of significant ways as: living, creator, redeemer, holy, lord, king, father, lover, savior, friend, provider, sustainer, deliverer, reconciler, teacher, peace-maker, comforter, judge, angry, hateful, warrior, wrathful, punisher, vindictive, vengeful, jealous, destructive, regretful, remorseful, grudging, just, righteous, steadfast, merciful, glorious, faithful, kind, good, understanding, eternal, everlasting, ever-present, all-wise, all-knowing, all-mighty, all-loving, etc. In an adequate systematic theology many of these adjectives and nouns, appellatives, are discussed as "the attributes of God." In my opinion, these descriptions of God can most adequately be interpreted in relationship to the God who is love revealed in Jesus Christ. Of course, this is no easy task but it is the number one issue in the development of the doctrine of God in a systematic theology and the interpretation of God in teaching and preaching the Gospel of the kingdom of God in the churches and to all humankind.

4. Reflections on the Topical Method

In each book of the Bible and in many passages some or all of the six components of the relational model are discussed and interpreted. A thorough study of the Bible may impart important knowledge of these six relationships. Every passage in the Bible is related in some fashion to each of these six relationships with their negative and positive qualities and their possible fulfillment in the norm of the revelation in Jesus Christ and the kingdom of God in history and eternity.

A similar approach to love as a critical principle is shown in the life and thought of Dr. John Nash. Nash's concept of "governing dynamics" is described in the movie *A Beautiful Mind*. The concept is that when all parties benefit from their involvements in a particular project, all parties win and no party loses. Professor Nash interprets this principle as an adequate critique and correction of Adam Smith's *Wealth of Nations* (1776). The concept of governing dynamics emerges when the texts of the Bible describe harmonious and constructive relationships in the six components of the relational model according to the revelation of God who is love in Jesus Christ. Dr. Nash comes to the conclusion in his studies and experiences of life that love is what is real and love is the primary analogy for reality. He believes that reason and mathematics can carry him only so far and that love is the real meaning of life. Other than love for his wife, I do not know Professor Nash's norm for the love to which he is committed. However, his approach is analogous to our critical principle of the God who is love revealed in Jesus Christ.

A summary of the topical study of the Bible with God as the topic may be helpful. This kind of biblical study is not easy. If it were easy, perhaps more Christians would be doing it. Even if the topic one chooses is an insignificant one, such as hairstyles, the study of the Bible regarding that topic will require much hard work. In the study of God, I have discussed each of the six components of the relational model from the perspective of a revelatory realism disclosed in Jesus Christ. Therefore, this relational realism is rooted and grounded in the normative revelation in Jesus Christ that God is love. You may follow this example and relate the topic you choose to the norm of the revelation in Jesus Christ in all of the relevant components of the relational model.

E. The Expository Method for Studying the Bible:
A Study of Mark 12:28-34

1. A Description of the Expository Method

Exposition is setting forth the meaning of something. The expository method of studying the Bible is often practiced along side of and along with the topical method. A major difference in these two methods is the attention focused on one topic in the topical method and the attention given to several topics in greater detail in the expository method. A second difference in the expository method is that significant attention is given to the general and particular contexts of the biblical passage. A third difference is that the text chosen is often studied more intensively in terms of its authorship, textual accuracy, type of literature, the characters, meanings of words, sentences, the passage itself and relationships to the writing or book where the text is located.

A study of the text is often described as an exegesis (Gk. *exegesis*, an interpretation, an explanation) or an exegetical approach. An exegesis is a critical explanation of a text or portion of the Bible with an awareness of one's own presuppositions or assumptions. Hermeneutics (Gr. *hermeneutike*, principles) is the study of the presuppositions and theological principles employed to guide an exegesis of a biblical passage. I am clearly engaging in hermeneutics and exegesis in this book. On pages 7-15, I discuss my hermeneutics (presuppositions and principles of interpretation) for studying the Bible. Then, I use my hermeneutics in the interpretation (exegesis) in both the topical and expository methods of studying the Bible. An expository method, however, often involves a more intensive and detailed study (exegesis) of a biblical text than a topical method which may involve the study of several passages in a more cursory way.

The exposition of the meaning of a biblical text in harmony with a norm, critical principle, principle of the closeness of relationships and a relational model is a challenging exercise involving both hermeneutics and exegesis. In serious study of the Bible, whether we are aware of it or not, we bring with us our perspectives, presuppositions and tools. Discuss in your notebook what you are bringing to your study of the Bible. If you are aware of the perspectives, presuppositions and tools you bring to biblical studies, your study of the Bible may be more fruitful and rewarding.

2. The General Context

In this guidebook, a study of an entire book of the Bible would probably be an unwieldy and unnecessary project. Therefore, Mark 12:28-34 is selected as an example of a significant passage to illustrate the expository method. Mark is probably the earliest of the synoptic Gospels (Mark, Matthew and Luke) and it was also written before the Gospel of John. Mark (John Mark) associated with Peter and Paul (Acts 12:12; 15:37-41; Col. 4:10; Philem. 24). In Christian tradition, he is thought to be the author of the Gospel of Mark in Rome before the fall of Jerusalem around A.D. 70. Apparently, Mark was greatly influenced by Peter and less so by Paul with whom he had a sharp disagreement at the beginning of Paul's second missionary journey (Acts 15:37-41).

Mark presents Jesus as the Son of God (1:1), the Son of Man (2:10) and the Messiah or Christ (1:1; 8:29) who is on an urgent (Gk. *euthus*, immediately; 1:12 and approximately 40 other references in Mark) mission from God involving the mighty works and significant teachings of Jesus. The theme of the message of Jesus is the kingdom of God (1:14-15) which is drawing near in him, his works and teachings including his parables and an eschatological (Gk. *ho eschatos*, the end time + *logos*, word) discourse in the thirteenth chapter (13:1-37) about the end time and the coming of the Son of Man. The mission and message of Jesus bring him into conflict with Jewish and Roman authorities. Jesus is charged, tried, convicted, condemned, beaten, crucified by the Romans, dies and is buried. On the third day, Jesus is reported to be raised from the dead (16:1-8).

There appear to be five major divisions in the Gospel of Mark. The first division describes the first events in the public life of Jesus with his baptism by John the Baptist followed by the temptation of Jesus by Satan (1:1-13). The second division presents the preaching, teaching and healing ministry of Jesus in Galilee (1:14-9:50). The third division describes the journey of Jesus from Galilee to Jerusalem (10:1-52). The fourth division presents the context for the passion narrative in the last week of his life ending in his crucifixion, death and burial (11:1-15:47). The fifth division of Mark describes the announcement of the resurrection of Jesus (16:1-8). The ending of Mark in 16:9-20 is absent from the earliest manuscripts. It is not regarded as written by Mark. At this point, it is important to read Mark 11:1-15:47 and record your major impressions about the general context for your study of this passage before you concentrate on Mark 12:28-34.

3. The Particular Context

If Mark 11:1-11 is chronologically and historically accurate as the entry of Jesus into Jerusalem on Palm Sunday, then the passage we are considering for our expository method of studying the Bible (Mark 12:28-34) occurs five days, or fewer, before the crucifixion of Jesus. On the day after Palm Sunday, Jesus went to the Temple and he began teaching in a hostile environment. As Jesus taught in this conflictive situation, he was challenged by a scribe (lawyer) who heard his disputations with others. The scribe approached Jesus and asked a difficult question perhaps for the scribe's enlightenment or as an attempt to trick and to embarrass Jesus.

The narrative is written by Mark and the speakers in our text are clearly identified as Jesus and an unnamed scribe. No scholar, to my knowledge, questions this account as an historical event with the dialogue reporting the actual words of Jesus and the scribe. We also know the narratives in the Gospels, especially Mark, are a unique kind of narrative literature. The immediate context of our text is the passion narrative of the last week in the life of Jesus. Throughout his messianic ministry, Jesus is well-known by Jews and Gentiles as The Teacher (Gk. *ho didaskalos*, teacher, rabbi) who engages in dialogue with Apostles, disciples, on-lookers, strangers and adversaries. It is important to remember the prominence of Jesus as Teacher especially in the midst of his passion, suffering and death. Jesus is addressed as The Teacher more often than by any other title. The particular context for our study of Mark 12:28-34, just described, will serve us well as we study the passage itself. At this point, it is important for you to read two additional translations of Mark 12:28-34 and to record your thoughts before reading any commentaries on this text.

4. An Expository Study of Mark 12:28-34

We have already learned that John Mark is the writer of the Gospel of Mark including Mark 12:28-34. Now, we examine this text regarding its authenticity in the earliest manuscripts. At this point, our tools serve us well since we have excellent commentaries in which the results of the examination of the texts are reported. The commentary on Mark in *The Interpreter's Bible*, vol. 7, pages 629-917, deals with textual differences as they arise in the exegesis of Mark and in every verse and passage in his sixteen chapters. No significant textual problem is connected with the text of Mark 12:28-34 (See pages 846-49) and this simplifies our study considerably.

Jesus is accustomed to rather heated controversies with Jewish religious leaders. In this situation, however, the controversial element appears to be modest and muted. Also, many people admire and appreciate Jesus even though they are not his disciples. The scribe thinks Jesus is answering questions well and he does not hesitate to ask his question. Jesus does not appear to be offended by the scribe as he takes his question at face value. Later, when Jesus sees that the scribe answers him wisely, he commends the scribe saying, "you are not far from the kingdom of God" (12:34b). It is interesting and important that in the midst of his passion, Jesus returns to the theme of his ministry and he addresses the scribe as a candidate for entering the kingdom of God. Mark gives singular attention to the kingdom of God and the Son of Man which now come into eschatological (end time) focus with the impending death of Jesus.

The Jews and their neighbors were well-aware of the Ten Commandments and the Jewish preoccupation with commandments and legal moral behavior as exhibited by some of the Pharisees. The priority of commandments was a serious matter and brevity was very desirable for the ordinary Jew. Jesus appears to be the first Jew to summarize the commandments in two commandments. Every pious Jew was aware of the first commandment Jesus gave since it is from Deuteronomy 6:4-5 and devout Jews quoted it both morning and evening as a prayer, the daily Shema.

A detailed exegesis of the first commandment would be lengthy but it is too important to be entirely ignored. The two names for God are most significant. In the Hebraic tradition, a name is much more than a means of identification. Name has to do with the character of a person or thing in itself. Lord (Heb. *Yahweh*) was the special name revealed to Moses (Ex. 3:13-15) and it was the most holy name for the God of the Hebrews and, after the Exile, the Jews. *Elohim*, (Heb., pl.) was the general name for God and it was translated by the Greek *ho theos*. Jesus accepted and affirmed the uniqueness of the Hebrew name for God as the perspective from which to describe, in part, the God revealed in him. The concept that God is one involves understanding diversity in the midst of unity (L. e pluribus unum). This concept is based on the Hebrew view of the extension of individual selfhood in the midst of corporate selfhood since all people are interrelated.

The second part of this first commandment (12:30), loving God with all your heart, soul, mind and strength, is a description of loving God with all that constitutes an individual as a person, that is, the totality of one's self. The word translated "love" in both the first and second commandments has a unique meaning in both Hebrew and Greek. The Greek infinitive is *agapein* and it means to love with an unqualified affection. Humans are to have an unqualified affection for God, for neighbor and for one's self. There is no need to add any comment, but the scribe could not forego his unique opportunity. After the scribe commended the answer Jesus gave to his question, he presumed to summarize the two commandments in his own words and add that it ". . . is much more than all whole burnt offerings and sacrifices" (12:33b). Jesus made no response.

The second commandment given by Jesus is a quotation from Leviticus 19:18b. The neighbor is anyone who is in need of the basic resources for survival and relief from oppression, suffering and distress. Jesus summarizes and unites the two great commandments. The basis for unity is the God who is love revealed to the Hebrews, Jews and to the Apostles and the disciples of Jesus Christ. This kind of love is the key to understanding the kingdom of God which Jesus told the scribe he was not far from entering. Divine love is a creative and redeeming love which embraces all imperfect forms and expressions of love and sanctifies, redeems and transforms them. Then, they become transparent to the love of God. This kind of love is who God is and is revealed to be in a normative way in Jesus. God is love and this love is reality itself. Forgiveness of and reconciliation to the neighbor are the hallmarks of the love of God revealed in Jesus Christ.

Mark wrote about the immediate effect of the dialogue between Jesus and the scribe, "And after that no one dared ask him any question" (12:34c). Even though Jesus was not questioned again in his public ministry, he was questioned and abused by the Jewish and Roman authorities before he was condemned to die by Pontus Pilate and then crucified by the Roman soldiers.

As we review the exposition of Mark 12:28-34 and apply our six components of the relational model, five of them are prominent in the narrative.

The I-It relationship is assumed and implied in "all whole burnt offerings and sacrifices" (12:33c). List in your notebook the six components of the relational model which you find in Mark 12:28-34 and relate them to the God who is love revealed in Jesus Christ. What does this biblical passage mean to you and for your life?

5. Reflections on the Expository Method

An expository study of the books of the Bible in a series is a plan which Christians can design and implement in order to educate themselves through the institutional churches, small groups and other organizations. The history of Christian education discloses that Christians who are well-educated in the Bible and the Christian Faith have seized the initiative and done most of it themselves. One successful approach in educating Christians in the content and meaning of the Bible is through an exposition of individual books, or passages, of the Bible in small groups.

The expository method can be employed at different levels. One level takes the text in any native language and interprets it without extensive research. Another level involves a thorough study of the text itself with attention to how Hebrew and Greek scholars interpret the text and its context. This may be described as an expository-textual method of study. The expository method in this guidebook tends toward an expository-textual study of the Bible. Of course, you or the members of your small study group decide at the outset the intensity level of your study.

The contents of the Bible are usually amenable to being outlined for study. Difficult texts can be dealt with in an outline which is somewhat more imposed than an outline which emerges from the text. *The Interpreter's Bible* provides an outline of each book and some helpful suggestions concerning the history and structure of the text. Once you get the hang of outlining books of the Bible, it becomes a creative, interesting and enlightening learning and teaching tool. Before you begin to outline a book of the Bible or read other materials about the book, read the book itself and record your thoughts in your notebook. Then, you gain your understanding of the book before your knowledge is slanted and reshaped by other information and ideas.

Read background material about a book (See *The New Westminster Dictionary of the Bible*) and read again the book for a more adequate overview. Record your general impressions in your working notes. Then, begin to investigate the text more analytically and see if the material falls naturally into a helpful outline. You will be pleasantly surprised at how easy this works and how much you are learning. Soon you will find how helpful the components of the relational model are in interpreting the text.

This example of the expository method of studying the Bible and the preceding example of the topical method, with God as the topic, serve as two primary ways of engaging in serious study of the Bible. It is important not to underestimate the hard work necessary to studying the Bible beneficially. The Bible is not a spiritual recipe book. The contents of the Bible have to do with God, creation and humankind and these subjects are not easy to understand in any academic discipline. Theology and philosophy are disciplines which ordinarily intend to deal with all reality. We often desire and expect a workable shortcut to genuine knowledge of reality. There are no satisfactory shortcuts in the study of theology, philosophy, the arts and sciences or the Bible.

F. Other Methods for Reading and Studying the Bible

There are many ways of reading and studying the Bible. To accomplish the goal of this guidebook, five ways of reading and studying the Bible are presented. Also, two methods of interpretation are described and illustrated. In the history of Western Civilization (Greek and Roman), numerous approaches to the study of documents are set forth and described as methods and types of exegesis. Edwin Cyril Blackman sets forth a history of the methods of studying the Bible in *Biblical Interpretation* (1957). This is not the place to review or to critique this history but it may be helpful for you to be aware of this informative source.

1. The Allegorical Method

We considered at length the topical and expository methods for studying the Bible. The allegorical method is a very different approach for studying the Bible. This method also played an important role in biblical interpretation in the early churches. It is still used often with the topical method in teaching and preaching the parables of Jesus and other difficult topics and texts. The Greek infinitive, *allegorein*, means to describe one thing in terms of the image of another. An allegory is a prolonged metaphor in which a series of actions are typically symbolic of other actions usually in a poetic or narrative form. John Bunyan's *Pilgrim's Progress* is an excellent example of an allegory in a narrative form. This literary form is used periodically in the Bible. Paul uses it in Galatians 4:21-31 and 1 Corinthians 10:1-4 but his major method is exegetical or rabbinic.

In the allegorical method, the primary use of a text is not concerned with what the text says and means in itself. Rather, the text serves as a base or point of reference for teaching an idea which the interpreter wishes to convey as valid and truthful. With the allegorical method Clement and Origen of Alexandria, Christian scholars in the Second and Third Centuries, were able to interpret difficult passages such as the adultery of David (2 Sam. 11:2-5) as teaching a commendable truth. Obviously, the allegorical method does not take seriously the actual meaning of a text. With this method any text can be used as an authority to teach anything one desires to teach. Therefore, I am not including the allegorical method as a viable option since it does not take the text itself seriously.

2. A List of Other Methods

In addition to the topical, expository and allegorical methods, there is an array of so-called methods for studying the Bible. The historical-critical method became prominent in the Nineteenth Century in *The Life of Jesus* (1835) by David Strauss. This method has a concern for the factual character of reported historical events such as the death of Jesus. It is also concerned with literary forms such as the parables of Jesus in the synoptic Gospels and the apocalyptic discourses in Mark and Revelation. In studying the Bible it is important to use some information and insights provided by a historical-critical approach to the Bible. Actually, there are as many variations of the historical-critical method as there are scholars who propose and embrace them. There are many "historical-critical" methods and the value of each method is determined in terms of its own hermeneutics and merits.

Do not be surprised when you encounter other methods or approaches to biblical studies. A few are listed here but not discussed. Documentary, textual, literary, form, redaction, structuralism, post-modern criticism and other approaches contribute to a comprehensive context for reading and studying the Bible today. With an awareness of and some input from these methods, we continue this project with a more modest and general approach to studying the Bible without getting bogged down in these important approaches which are less relevant for this guidebook.

G. Begin Your Study with
What Interests You Most in the Bible

Obviously, you have some interest in the Bible since you are reading this book. Think carefully about your primary interest and describe in your notebook your honest, genuine and untampered-with interest in the Bible. Is your interest identified as a wholesome and legitimate one, a Godly interest, which is important enough to motivate you over a long period of time to devote your time, energy and resources to an intensive study of the Bible? Or, are you just surfing religious sources and looking for some miraculous short-cut, quick-fix solution to your problems? If you have a burning and irrepressible passion for studying the Bible, no one can stop you. If you can take it or leave it alone, no one can persuade you to study the Bible seriously.

Begin where you are now in reading and studying the Bible. For example, let us suppose that you read the Bible devotionally and in preparation for your Sunday School or Church School classes. As you engage in these exercises, apply just one, two or three of the tools described in this guidebook and see what you learn. As you become comfortable with this level of study use other tools. Tool eight is activated when you begin your plan for reading and studying the Bible. If you are content with your first level, be pleased and happy with it. If you desire to move to another level, proceed at your own speed and enjoy your study of the Bible. You do not fail in reading and studying the Bible at any level if you meet the goals which you set.

One additional suggestion may become very helpful to you in understanding and using this guidebook. Everyone knows how to "doodle" which means to play around with in an open and relaxed manner. One of the best ways for you to understand this book is to doodle around with a pencil, pen, or crayon when you read, for example, about the "circle of faith" or the relational model. Many concepts and ideas in this book can be partially expressed in diagrams, images, sketches, and pictures of various kinds. In my studies and teaching, I use dots, arrows, circles, arcs, ellipses, cones (funnels), inverted cones, lines, segments, squares, rectangles, two-dimensional diagrams, three-dimensional diagrams and an uninhibited imagination. I try to visualize reality from the smallest to the largest, from the universal to the particular and to reflect on my relationships to everything and everyone. The graphic (The Relational Model) on page 27 is a direct result of my "doodling" over several decades in teaching systematic theology. Read this book again and begin with your doodling pad as you work through it. Try it and I think you will like it! In theology and philosophy, there is a spatial, temporal and mathematical dimension analogous to those in the physical and social sciences.

1. The Topical Method: Your First Exercise

After you select your topic, take your Bible, a dictionary, concordance, workbook, and this guidebook and go to work. Soon you may discover that the topic you chose is not the one you really want to study or that this topic is so complex that you are not ready to study it. Also, there are many topics and questions which are not addressed or answered in the Bible. For example, Jesus does not know the answers to all questions (Mk. 13:32). Thus, getting started in itself is not easy. Topics often studied are: creation, humankind, image of God, evil, sin, promises of God, covenants, Ten Commandments, God the Father, Jesus the Christ and Son of God, God the Holy Spirit, worship, the Apostles, biblical personalities, forgiveness, reconciliation, discipleship, salvation, redemption, recapitulation, prophecy, Sermon on the Mount, justice, suffering, punishment, the Christian life, justification, sanctification, glorification, death, resurrection, kingdom of God, church, heaven, hell and the life everlasting. Make your first effort with a carefully selected topic and share your work with a small group of interested friends. When the study is finished, write a summary of the benefits of the study for you and share it with your study group.

2. The Expository Method: Your Second Exercise

Choosing a passage from a book in the Bible for exposition may be easier than selecting a topic. Immediately, you have a text with which to work. For Christians, it is important to begin the study of the Bible with primary attention to the New Testament, especially the synoptic Gospels and Acts. As indicated, I recommend first the study of Mark, then Luke, Acts, Matthew and John. Discuss with friends the selection of a book or passage for your expository study and, when finished, summarize the benefits of your study. Some of the shorter books I suggest are: 1 John, 1 Peter, Philippians, Galatians, Ephesians, Colossians, 1 and 2 Thessalonians, 1 and 2 Timothy, Titus and Jude. The book of Revelation comes last in the Bible and it will be easier if you study it later rather than earlier. After this first exercise, make a plan for additional studies in the more lengthy books of the New Testament and the books of the Old Testament.

3. Reflections on Methods for Studying the Bible

Now that you have firsthand experience in reading and studying the Bible using the topical and expository methods presented in this guidebook, your eyes may be opened to additional possibilities and benefits from reading and studying the Bible for the rest of your life.

It is exceedingly important to remember several matters regarding methods. Method (Gk. *meta*, after + *hodos*, way) means to follow a particular way or path in pursuing a goal. First, a method is simply a way of studying which is imposed on the text or data. Second, all methods rearrange and skew the subject-matter. Third, there is no perfect method but some methods are more adequate than others. Fourth, methods tend to overlap and modify one another as seen in our discussions of the topical and expository methods. Fifth, every method is based on presuppositions regarding a norm and a critical principle for interpreting the norm, that is, hermeneutics. Sixth, when employing any method we must review our work periodically to ascertain whether we have drifted away from our method in essential ways. "Method drift" will skew the results of any method and impoverish its findings and conclusions. Seventh, when disciples of Jesus Christ read and study the Bible, adequate methods have personal value only if the results of the studies motivate disciples to grow in the grace and knowledge of the Lord Jesus Christ and the God who is love revealed in Jesus of Nazareth. Presuppositions and methods, in large measure, determine the outcome of any endeavor. If you know your presuppositions and methodology, your study of the Bible may be coherent and inspirational. Your daily life as a disciple connected to the Lord Jesus Christ will bring you tremendous knowledge, wisdom and joy. An important question to ask every morning is "What will be my discipleship-connection to Jesus Christ today?" The goal of this book (p. ix) is to make available a cluster of useful tools (presuppositions and methodology) which will enable readers to know and enjoy the God who is love through their connections to the Lord Jesus Christ.

IV
AT HOME IN THE BIBLE

I have always felt at home in the Bible. But I did not know how to read and to study the Bible satisfactorily until I was a graduate student in theology at The Southern Baptist Theological Seminary. Professor Eric C. Rust taught me to approach the Bible, especially the Old Testament, from the perspective of the normative revelation of God in Jesus Christ. The contents of the Bible became more fully related and understood. The many books became one book—the Holy Bible.

You do not need to go to graduate school in theology to be able to study the Bible in ways which make sense in harmony with your confession of faith that Jesus Christ is your Lord and Savior. You may need to reexamine some of your approaches to and theories about the Bible which may be keeping you in the dark. If you follow the "way to go about it" described in this guidebook, the contents of the Bible may soon begin to open up like a giant sunflower. Automatically, you will be relating the passages you are reading to the revelation in Jesus Christ. You will begin to appreciate each part of the Bible in its own immediate context and its importance in itself. Then, you will soon rearrange the role and relevance of all passages in the Bible according to how you see all things from the perspective of the God who is love revealed in Jesus Christ.

Continue to review and to revise your plan while being careful not to depart from the norm of the revelation in Jesus Christ. Bring the Bible into your daily life and through diligent study and prayer enable it to become your Bible. The Holy Spirit will be your teacher and guide. God's speed and blessings on you as you "think through what it means to be a Christian" during your Christian pilgrimage. The Apostles thought through what it meant for them to be disciples of Jesus Christ and, among other things, the kingdom of God became manifest, Pentecost happened, Christian churches began and the New Testament came to be written. The Apostles and other disciples "thought through" the revelation of God in Jesus Christ and the New Testament is the written form of their responses to this revelation. Only time will tell what the results may be from your seeking the mind of Christ as you think through what being a Christian means to you and for your I-Self relationship. Only you can do this for yourself with God's help; therefore, see to it that you permit no one else to do it for you since you are now free in Christ (Gal. 5:1). When you fall in love with God, you discover who you are in relationship to yourself, everyone and everything. You feel at home in the Bible. Your home is the kingdom of God now and forever.

I have examined many views of God, the universe and the meaning of life. There appears to me to be no worthy substitute for the God who is love. I pray daily that I will never again forget the God who is love. God's love neither ends and nor fails (1 Cor. 13:8). God's love is always better than hate, rage and self-pity. It is better to be loving than it is to be to be right or perfect. "So faith, hope, love abide, these three, but the greatest of these is love" (1 Cor. 13:13). "Make love your aim" (1 Cor. 14:1a)! The love of God being revealed in the face of Jesus Christ is the light of the world (2 Cor. 4:6), the hope for everyone and everything, and God's greatest love gift to you and to the world (Jn.3:16; Rom 6:23; 1 Jn. 4:8, 16).

NOTES

NOTES

NOTES

NOTES

NOTES